11+

Success

for CEM

Comprehension

Results Booster

Results Booster

Angela Marks

Contents

Guidance for Parents

About the 11+ tests

In most cases, the 11+ selection tests are set by GL Assessment (NFER), CEM (The University of Durham) or the individual school. You should be able to find out which tests your child will be taking on the website of the school they are applying to, or from the local authority.

The CEM test consists of two papers and in each paper pupils are tested on their abilities in verbal, non-verbal and numerical reasoning. Tests are separated into small, timed sections delivered by audio instructions. It appears the content required for CEM tests changes from year to year, and the level at which pupils are tested, ranges from county to county.

For pupils to do well in the CEM tests:

- They must have strong arithmetic skills

- They must have strong reasoning and problem-solving skills

- They must have a strong core vocabulary

- They must be flexible and able to understand and respond to a wide range of question types and formats, without being panicked by unfamiliar question types

- They must be able to work under time pressure.

This book provides preparation for the verbal reasoning aspect of the exam and, more specifically, for reading comprehension. Children must read a passage and then respond to a series of multiple-choice questions by choosing the correct option. These tests assess children's vocabulary and understanding of a passage as well as their reading speed and accuracy.

The importance of practice

Practice will help your child to do his or her best on the day of the tests. Working through the more difficult question types allows your child to practise answering a range of test-style questions that will help them achieve the best results. It also provides an opportunity to learn how to manage time effectively, so that time is not wasted during the test and any 'extra' time is used constructively for checking.

How to prepare for the 11+ tests

- Use this book to help your child get used to answering questions under time constraints

- Help your child revise and practise problem areas

- Help your child gain confidence in their abilities

- Talk about coping with pressure

- Let your child know that tests are just one part of school life

- Let them know that doing their best is what matters

- Plan a fun incentive for after the 11+ tests, such as a day out

Comprehension Test 1

 INSTRUCTIONS

 You have 6 minutes to complete the following exercise.
You have 10 questions to complete within the time given.

Read the passage and answer the questions that follow.

EXAMPLE

Anne bought some new slippers yesterday. They are red with pretty little bows at the front.

What colour are Anne's new slippers?

A Pink

B Blue

C Purple

(D) Red

E Brown

The correct answer is **D**.

School Rules

If I were a head teacher in charge of a school, things would be different – oh yes they would! No more misery, no more punishments, no more boredom, and here's what I would do.

There would be just five rules to remember and everyone would have to learn them and everyone must swear to keep those rules. The first rule and the most important one is the rule of kindness. This is the Golden Rule and it goes something like this: You will be kind to everyone, at all times, always and forever. You will say to each person and inside your head, "How may I help you?" or "What is it I can do for you?" and "How can I make your day better?"

Now for rule number two: You don't have to wear a uniform – no way! You can wear what you want every day and everyone must enjoy and admire the wonderful variety of outfits worn by the pupils.

Rule number three is about being creative. Human beings are born to be creative, to invent and discover and to create a multitude of things. Every day will be spent following your creative thoughts. Rule number three says you must seek to create and at the end of the day you must smile and say, "today I have created this or crafted that and tomorrow I will design something different."

Rule four is about relaxation. Yes, that's right. In my school there would be a very strict rule that you must chill out, calm down, have some quiet time or even put your feet up. This blissful rest would be compulsory. Four times a day for 20 minutes at the least. During these rest periods, soft pillows would be provided, but no snoring or dribbling!

Finally, rule five is to be happy and your success at school would be measured by how happy you are and how happy you make others, especially your teachers. The teachers would count only smiles and laughter and put that on your school report.

1 Which phrase has the same meaning as 'Everyone must swear to keep the rules'?
   A   Everyone would say very rude words
   B   Everyone would promise to keep the rules
   C   Everyone would shout the rules
   D   Everyone would forget the rules
   E   Everyone would change the rules

2 Which rule does the author call the Golden Rule?
   A   Rule two
   B   Rule four
   C   Rule five
   D   Rule three
   E   Rule one

3 What does the author mean by the words 'Golden Rule?'
   A   It is the most important rule of all
   B   It is written in gold letters
   C   It is the hardest rule to keep
   D   If you keep this rule, you get a golden ruler as a prize
   E   You get a gold star for keeping this rule

4 Which word is similar in meaning to 'variety'?
   A   Collection
   B   Amount
   C   Group
   D   Mixture
   E   Design

Go to the next page.

(5) Which phrase best describes rule number three?

A   Don't waste time making things

B   You must do an art class every day

C   Being creative is important and you must make something every day

D   This is a rule about creating a picture

E   This rule says you must make stuff even if you don't want to

(6) What type of word is 'relaxation'?

A   Pronoun

B   Verb

C   Adjective

D   Simile

E   Noun

(7) In rule four, what are you not allowed to do?

A   Put your feet up

B   Sing

C   Snore

D   Rest

E   Calm down

(8) Which word is similar in meaning to 'compulsory'?

A   Essential

B   Unnecessary

C   Allowed

D   Optional

E   Definite

(9) Which word is similar in meaning to 'measured'?

A   Written

B   Judged

C   Obstructed

D   Prevented

E   Posted

(10) What will be recorded on the school report?

A   Behaviour points

B   Head teacher's awards

C   Sporting trophies

D   Maths tests

E   Smiles

Comprehension Test 2

 You have 6 minutes to complete the following exercise.
You have 10 questions to complete within the time given.

Read the passage and answer the questions that follow.

The Railway Children

The story begins with Phyllis, Peter and their older sister Roberta, known affectionately as Bobbie, recalling a summer some years ago when they were 8, 10 and 12 respectively.

It had all begun when two official-looking men had arrived at their London home. Father, who worked for the government, was arrested and charged with spying. The children were unaware of the reasons behind their father's absence and their mother didn't want to tell them where he had gone.

Without their father's income, they had become very poor and Mother told the children they were going to live in Yorkshire. The family's new home was a small stone cottage called Three Chimneys, which was situated close to a railway line and a railway station. The children liked to stand in the fields and wave to the train passengers and from one of the carriages, the same old man would always wave back.

Peter, keen to help his mother and aware that they had very little money, stole coal from the station yard, but he was caught by Perks the porter. The children were very sorry and told him about the family's struggles. Mr Perks forgave them and they became friends.

One day the children went as usual to wave to the passengers on the train and particularly the old gentlemen. They noticed a landslide had completely blocked the tracks and, knowing the train was due to arrive, they realised they had to warn the driver. The girls took off their red petticoats and waved them in front of the oncoming train. The train stopped and an accident was prevented. The old gentleman rewarded them with gold pocket watches and at the end of the story, the same old gentleman cleared their father's name of spying charges and he returned to his family.

Go to the next page.

1 What had happened to Father?

   A   He had gone for a walk

   B   He had gone to the office

   C   He had gone with his friends

   D   He had run away

   E   He had been arrested

2 Why didn't Mother tell the children where their father had gone?

   A   She didn't want to worry them

   B   She didn't know where he had gone

   C   She was glad he'd gone

   D   She knew he would be back soon

   E   She thought the children might look for him

3 Why did Peter steal the coal?

   A   He wanted to play with it

   B   He wanted to be a coal miner

   C   He wanted to help his Mother as they were now poor

   D   He knew it would annoy Mr Perks

   E   He knew it would annoy his mother

4 How did Perks feel when he found out Peter had stolen the coal?

   A   He kept the information to himself

   B   He wanted to report him to the police

   C   When he heard their story, he forgave them

   D   He was furious and told their mother

   E   He ignored the theft

5 Which word is similar in meaning to 'struggles'?

   A   History

   B   Fears

   C   Heirlooms

   D   Problems

   E   Celebrations

6 Why did the girls use their red petticoats to alert the train driver?

  A   They felt too hot

  B   They couldn't run easily wearing petticoats

  C   Red represents danger and is easily seen

  D   They needed to step over the railway tracks

  E   They needed to climb the embankment

7 Why did the children stop the train?

  A   They needed to get on it

  B   They wanted to speak to the old gentleman

  C   The train was too early

  D   They were being naughty

  E   There was a landslide on the line

8 How did the old gentleman reward the children?

  A   With free tickets for the train

  B   With gold pocket watches

  C   With a medal

  D   He shook their hands

  E   He just said thank you

9 What does the phrase 'cleared their father's name' mean?

  A   Father's name could be changed

  B   Father's name had been rubbed out

  C   Father had been found guilty of a crime

  D   Father's name had to be written in a different way

  E   The truth had been established and Father was innocent

10 What did Father do after he had been released from prison?

  A   He took a holiday

  B   He ran away

  C   He caught the train

  D   He returned to his family

  E   He got a new job

Comprehension Test 3

 You have 10 minutes to complete the following exercise. You have 10 questions to complete within the time given.

Read the passage and answer the questions that follow.

Bloody Bush Mountain Bike Trail

The Kielder Forest is actually six forests in one, but this forest is not just about trees. One quarter of the area of the Kielder Forest is in fact open space which includes England's largest area of blanket bog.

Blanket bog is an area of peatland formed where there is a climate of very high rainfall and the peat, which looks like thick black soil, develops over large expanses of gently rolling ground.

Surrounding this boggy area is the breathtaking Kielder Forest which is a large man-made woodland. Many of these trees have been planted as part of the Forestry Commission's planting programme and were originally intended to be cut down and used for timber.
Timber is harvested annually and is supplied to local sawmills for chipboard, pulp and wood fuel. Once the trees are cut down, the open areas are replanted with a mix of conifers and broad-leaved trees.

A breathtaking adventure ride for mountain bikes, the 20-mile Bloody Bush trail takes the rider through some of the UK's wildest terrain. The trail is named after a location on the Scottish border where, in medieval times, a pitched battle occurred between English cattle raiders and Scottish herdsmen. Here there is an area of open moorland where cattle still graze today.

The trail itself is a difficult one. The rider must take into account that it is one of the most remote places in England and the weather can turn rapidly from sunshine to a blizzard. An accident here, or even a simple wrong turning, could have very serious consequences and for this reason the rider must be well prepared.

A mountain bike is a bicycle created for off-road cycling. These types of bicycles are typically ridden on mountain trails but are in fact all-terrain cycles. Mountain bikes differ from a typical bicycle in many ways and the most notable differences are the suspension on the framework, larger knobbly tyres, very durable heavy wheels, lower gear ratio needed for steep gradients and more powerful brakes.

Preparing the bike carefully before starting out is a must. Check the bike thoroughly – brakes, tyres, chain and pedals – and be sure to remember important items such as a whistle, torch, change of clothing, lots of water and of course lunch! Make sure you tell someone where you are going and when you are due back.

The trail itself is very wet and boggy and has patches of peat so the surface of the trail has to be prepared to allow bikes to get through. This is done by laying stones and wooden slats over the wettest and boggiest areas. Mountain bikes are built to handle this type of terrain and to move with some ease through loose sand, loose gravel, roots and rocks.

The rider needs to be experienced in a wide range of climbs and descents and able to cope with surfaces such as boardwalks, beams, large rocks, medium steps, drop-offs, cambers and water crossings.

The sport became popular in the 1970s in Northern California, USA, where riders rode down the rugged hillsides. A bicycle-frame builder called Joe Breeze developed the first mountain bike and in 2006 a documentary film was produced examining this period of off-road cycling in detail, called *Klunkerz: A Film About Mountain Bikes*. By the 2000s, mountain biking had moved from a little-known sport to an activity complete with an international racing circuit and a world championship.

Mountain biking is popular with both males and females and events are held for juniors as well as seniors. One of the largest mountain-bike events is the World Cup held at Fort William in Scotland where 250 riders from 25 nations, representing the world's best downhillers, all descend on Fort William to compete for this championship.

Go to the next page.

1. Which phrase best explains 'A breathtaking adventure'?

   A   A very difficult expedition

   B   A tough challenge

   C   An exhausting event

   D   A thrilling and exciting experience

   E   A restful hike

2. What does the author mean by 'the UK's wildest terrain'?

   A   A place with dangerous people

   B   A remote and desolate land

   C   A place where you can have lots of fun

   D   A place where there are wild animals

   E   A very windy area

3. What does the phrase 'serious consequences' mean?

   A   The rider will have to pay a fine

   B   The rider might be punished

   C   The rider might be told off

   D   The rider's parents would be very angry

   E   The effect of not preparing properly could be very serious

4. Why must the rider be well prepared?

   A   It is a very remote place with rapidly changing weather

   B   There are no restaurants so they will have to have a picnic

   C   The rider will need to go to the toilet before leaving

   D   The days are always sunny so they need sun cream

   E   They will need money to buy a burger

5. Why does the author write: 'Make sure you tell someone where you are going and when you are due back'?

   A   The person may want to come with you

   B   The person may want to meet up with you

   C   The person wants to wave to you

   D   The person will get help if you don't come back at the right time

   E   The person wants their bike back

(6) Which word is similar in meaning to 'boggy'?

A   Stony

B   Slippery

C   Marshy

D   Grassy

E   Slimy

(7) How are the surfaces of the trail prepared for bike riding?

A   Tarmac is laid

B   Concrete paths are made

C   A bike lane is marked out

D   Stones and wooden planks are laid down

E   No preparation is required

(8) What does the phrase 'wide range of climbs and descents' mean?

A   Lots of different types of hills and drops

B   A large expanse of moorland

C   Many different types of vegetation

D   Many rock climbs along the way

E   Many high mountains

(9) Which word is similar in meaning to 'cope'?

A   Create

B   Ride

C   Manage

D   Develop

E   Cover

(10) What type of word is 'rider'?

A   Pronoun

B   Verb

C   Noun

D   Adjective

E   Collective noun

Comprehension Test 4

 You have 8 minutes to complete the following exercise.
You have 10 questions to complete within the time given.

Read the poem and answer the questions that follow.

For my Grandmother Knitting

There is no need they say
but the needles still move
their rhythms in the working of your hands
as easily
as if your hands
were once again those sure and skilful hands
of the fisher-girl.

You are old now
and your grasp of things is not so good
but master of your moments then
deft and swift
you slit the still-ticking quick silver fish.
Hard work it was too
of necessity.

But now they say there is no need
as the needles move
in the working of your hands
once the hands of the bride
with the hand-span waist
once the hands of the miner's wife
who scrubbed his back
in a tin bath by the coal fire
once the hands of the mother
of six who made do and mended
scraped and slaved slapped sometimes
when necessary.

But now they say there is no need
the kids they say grandma
have too much already
more than they can wear

too many scarves and cardigans-
gran you do too much
there's no necessity…

At your window you wave
them goodbye Sunday.
With your painful hands
big on shrunken wrists.
Swollen-jointed. Red. Arthritic. Old.
But the needles still move
their rhythms in the working of your hands
easily
as if your hands remembered
of their own accord the pattern
as if your hands had forgotten
how to stop.

Poem by Liz Lochhead

(1) What kind of work did grandmother used to do when she was younger?

    A   She was a weaver

    B   She was a jeweller

    C   She made knitted items

    D   She was a sailor

    E   She gutted fish

(2) What does the poet mean by the phrase 'your grasp of things is not so good'?

    A   Grandmother drops things

    B   Grandmother sometimes finds it hard to understand things

    C   Grandmother has arthritis

    D   Grandmother keeps dropping stitches

    E   Grandmother needs to use a walking stick

(3) What type of word is 'deft', in the second stanza?

    A   Noun

    B   Adjective

    C   Simile

    D   Adverb

    E   Pronoun

(4) What does the author mean by the phrase 'you slit the still-ticking quick silver fish'?

    A   The fish was clockwork

    B   She had a pet fish

    C   She enjoyed a fish supper

    D   She fed the fish

    E   She cut open the fish while it was still wriggling

Go to the next page.

5) What are the 'needles'?

    A   Pine tree needles

    B   Sewing needles

    C   Crochet needles

    D   Knitting needles

    E   Syringes

6) What is the meaning of the phrase 'with a hand-span waist'?

    A   Grandmother's waist was very small

    B   Grandmother had a lot of rubbish

    C   Grandmother had a large waist

    D   Grandmother wore a belt

    E   Grandmother didn't waste anything

7) What do the grandchildren say about their Grandmother's knitted items?

    A   They want more of them

    B   They love them

    C   They have enough cardigans and scarves

    D   Nothing

    E   They are worried about her health

8) What does the poet mean by the phrase 'With your painful hands big on shrunken wrists'?

    A   Grandmother had washed her hands too often

    B   Grandmother seemed to have very thin wrists because her hands were so swollen

    C   Grandmother had very big hands compared to her grandchildren

    D   Grandmother had been a miner

    E   Grandmother had big hands from too much knitting

9) Which word is similar in meaning to 'rhythm'?

    A   Massive

    B   Minute

    C   Beat

    D   Long

    E   Oval

10) What had Grandmother's hands forgotten?

    A   How to think

    B   How to remember

    C   How to stop

    D   How to search

    E   How to wash

INSTRUCTIONS

You have 10 minutes to complete the following exercise.
You have 10 questions to complete within the time given.

Read the passage and answer the questions that follow.

The Great Fire of London

The fire started at 1 a.m. on Sunday 2 September 1666 in Thomas Farriner's bakery on Pudding Lane. No one knows exactly how the fire started but it quickly spread to the nearby warehouses surrounding Pudding Lane.

The warehouses were full of highly flammable things like timber, rope and tar, and after a very long hot summer all the timbers of the buildings would have been very dry. A strong easterly wind blew the fire from building to building.

In 1979 archaeologists excavating the remains of a burnt-out shop in Pudding Lane discovered the charred remains of 20 barrels of pitch tar, which is very flammable material and would have helped the fire to gain hold.

Because the fire was spreading so quickly, most Londoners concentrated on escaping the flames rather than fighting the fires. Thomas Farriner and his family had to climb out of the upstairs window and onto the neighbour's roof to escape the flames.

Many people fled towards the river and tried to get on boats. Others tried to reach fields and open spaces, which in those days surrounded the city. Many people had to stay out in the countryside in tents and shelters for many days after the fire.

There wasn't a fire brigade in London in 1666 so the people themselves, helped by some soldiers, had to fight the fire. However, this didn't really work as the flames were leaping from roof to roof very quickly. Therefore, on the third day of the fire it was decided to destroy houses by blowing them up with gunpowder, so as to create a firebreak. This made a large empty space across which the fire couldn't spread.

King Charles II did not flee from the fire but stayed in London and took charge of the operation to save the city. The citizens and soldiers carried out King Charles' plan to create firebreaks. King Charles also ordered Navy supplies that were stored in the East End docks to be taken to those who had fled and were now living outside the city.

Go to the next page.

The greatest fear the authorities had was that the flames might cross the River Thames and set fire to the south side of the city. This was prevented by the weather. The wind that had helped the fire spread turned on itself, driving the flames back into the area that had already been burnt so that the fire had nothing to ignite. On 4 September the wind dropped and the firefighters finally gained control. By dawn on 6 September the last fires were out.

The Great Fire had burnt down 84 churches and the old St Paul's Cathedral. It had killed five people and damaged most of the homes and shops in London. However, it had also destroyed the filthy streets associated with the disease from the Great Plague, and had sterilised a river flowing into the Thames that had been nothing more than an open sewer. Therefore it could be said that the fire did London and its people a favour. It had destroyed this dirty city which was now able to be replanned and rebuilt.

The task of rebuilding the city's churches was given to Sir Christopher Wren who was a famous architect. Sir Christopher Wren built the churches on the footprint of the old ones. These churches had arches and beautiful stained-glass windows and he chose to design domes into the structure of the roofs. This was the case when he built a new St Paul's Cathedral which is now one of the most famous and recognisable sights of London. Its construction was completed in Wren's lifetime and has dominated the skyline for 300 years. This building survived a second fire of London known as the Blitz during the Second World War.

1. Which phrase explains 'highly flammable'?

   A   The flames were high

   B   Very dangerous

   C   Easily extinguished

   D   Easily set on fire

   E   Highly toxic

2. What helped the fire to spread so quickly?

   A   There wasn't a fire alarm

   B   The sprinklers didn't work

   C   The fire was very fierce

   D   The strong easterly wind

   E   Thunder and lightning

3. Which word is similar in meaning to 'excavate'?

   A   Evacuate

   B   Envelop

   C   Entered

   D   Excess

   E   Dig

4. How did Thomas Farriner's family escape?

   A   They climbed down a ladder

   B   They jumped out of a window

   C   They climbed onto the roof

   D   They climbed down the drainpipe

   E   They ran to the river

5. Which phrase best describes the city of London in 1666?

   A   A huge city with skyscrapers

   B   A city with closely built buildings and surrounded by countryside

   C   A small village next to a river

   D   A bustling seaside resort

   E   A quiet village in the countryside

Go to the next page.

6 How did most people escape the fire?

A   They ran to the river and jumped on a boat

B   They ran to the fire station

C   They ran into stone buildings

D   They left on horseback

E   They left on a stagecoach

7 What kind of temporary homes did some of the Londoners live in?

A   Sheds

B   Hotels

C   Chalets

D   Churches

E   Tents

8 Why weren't the Londoners able to put the fire out with water?

A   The flames were too fierce and the wind swept the flames along

B   The taps were too far away

C   The fire brigade were at another fire

D   They thought the fire was out but it wasn't

E   They thought the fire was less serious than it really was

9 How was a firebreak created?

A   The people fighting the fire had a cup of tea

B   The person in charge said they should take a break

C   The fire was put out with water

D   A large space was made by blowing up some houses

E   Gunpowder was put onto the fire

10 What does 'the wind dropped' mean?

A   The wind blew from the east

B   The wind lessened

C   The wind picked things up and dropped them

D   The wind increased in strength

E   The wind was blowing the trees

Comprehension Test 6

 You have 10 minutes to complete the following exercise.
You have 10 questions to complete within the time given.

Read the article and answer the questions that follow.

UK health experts call for ban on tackling in school rugby

More than 70 doctors and health experts have called for a ban on tackling in school rugby games.

In an open letter that warns of the high risk of serious injury among under-18s playing rugby, they urge schools to move to touch and non-contact versions of the game.

A government drive to boost participation in rugby in English schools by linking them with rugby clubs is also criticised by the health experts, who point out that the UN convention on the rights of the child obliges governments to inform children about injury risks.

The letter – which is addressed to ministers, chief medical officers and children's commissioners – describes rugby as a "high-impact collision sport".

"The majority of all injuries occur during contact or collision, such as the tackle and the scrum," it says. "These injuries, which include fractures, ligamentous tears, dislocated shoulders, spinal injuries and head injuries, can have short-term, life-long and life-ending consequences for children."

The letter is the first stage of a campaign that will include a petition on the change.org website which, if it receives 100 000 signatures, will trigger the consideration of a debate by MPs on the issue.

Rugby is a compulsory part of the physical education curriculum from the age of 11 in many boys' schools, particularly in the independent sector.

The letter, signed by sport scholars, academics, doctors and public health professionals, says repeat concussions have been found to have a link to cognitive impairment, and an association with problems such as depression, memory loss and diminished verbal abilities. Children also took longer to recover to normal levels on measures of memory, reaction speed and post-concussive symptoms.

Go to the next page.

Stating that children are being exposed to serious and catastrophic risk of injury, Prof Allyson Pollock (a professor of public health research and policy at Queen Mary University of London) said: "Parents expect the state to look after their children when they are at school. Rugby is a high-impact collision sport and given that children are more susceptible to injuries such as concussion, the absence of injury surveillance systems and primary prevention strategies is worrying."

Eric Anderson, a professor of sport, masculinities and sexualities at the University of Winchester, said the signatories did not have a contention with rugby, but with the collisions that occur in the sport.

"School children should not be forced to collide with other children as part of the national curriculum for physical education," he said. "A more sensible approach is to play tag rugby."

A Department for Education spokeswoman said schools were expected to be aware of the risks associated with sporting activities and to provide a safe environment for pupils.

"Team sports, such as rugby, play an important role in developing character," she said. "They can help children and young people develop positive traits, such as fair play, leadership and resilience, and teach them how to bounce back from defeat, how to respect others and how to work together in teams to achieve a goal.

"We have given schools the flexibility to organise and deliver a diverse and challenging PE curriculum which best suits the needs of their students."

The Rugby Football Union said it took player safety "extremely seriously" and that recent changes meant young players underwent a "gradual and managed" introduction to the contact version of the game.

A spokesman said the union had also carried out a three-year injury prevention and surveillance study on schoolboy injuries, as well as implementing a guidance programme known as RugbySafe. He added: "We believe that high quality coaching, officiating, medical support and appropriate player behaviour in line with the core values all contribute to reducing the risk of injury occurring."

Extract from: *The Guardian 2nd March 2016* by Ben Quinn

① Why are experts calling for a ban on tackling in rugby?

    A   They are all spoilsports

    B   They say tackling can cause serious injuries

    C   They want everyone to play basketball

    D   They think children should not be so aggressive

    E   They think children get too dirty

② Which word is similar in meaning to 'majority'?

    A   Majorette

    B   Achieve

    C   Few

    D   Most

    E   Win

③ What is meant by the word 'petition'?

    A   A competition

    B   A list of changes

    C   A list of signatures

    D   A list of experts

    E   A shopping list

④ In the phrase 'rugby is a compulsory part of the physical education curriculum', which word is similar in meaning to 'compulsory'?

    A   Comprehensive

    B   Required

    C   Clear

    D   Conformity

    E   Reactionary

⑤ What do the experts believe that parents expect from the government?

    A   That their children will be looked after at school

    B   That their children will be given regular exercise

    C   That their children will be allowed to choose

    D   That the state will never allow rugby

    E   That the teachers will not look after the children

Go to the next page.

6 What do the experts believe will be a sensible option to tackling in rugby?

A   Pig in the middle

B   Tin can squat

C   Kiss chase

D   Tag rugby

E   Tig

7 What type of word is 'curriculum'?

A   Adjective

B   Adverb

C   Pronoun

D   Noun

E   Verb

8 Which word is similar in meaning to 'resilience'?

A   Enjoyment

B   Toughness

C   Aggression

D   Fairness

E   Ability

9 What part of the game do the health experts think is too dangerous?

A   Rugby

B   Government

C   Enjoyment

D   Collisions

E   PE teachers

10 What is the attitude of the Rugby Football Union to the proposed changes?

A   They think rugby is perfectly safe

B   They are very careful about player safety

C   They just want to get on with the game

D   They supported the ban

E   They signed the petition

INSTRUCTIONS

You have 8 minutes to complete the following exercise.
You have 10 questions to complete within the time given.

Read the passage and answer the questions that follow.

The Little Princess

Once on a dark winter's day, when the yellow fog hung so thick and heavy in the streets of London that the lamps were lighted and the shop windows blazed with gas as they do at night, an odd-looking little girl sat in a cab with her father and was driven rather slowly through the big thoroughfares.

She sat with her feet tucked under her, and leaned against her father, who held her in his arm, as she stared out of the window at the passing people with a queer old-fashioned thoughtfulness in her big eyes.

She was such a little girl that one did not expect to see such a look on her small face. It would have been an old look for a child of twelve, and Sara Crewe was only seven. The fact was, however, that she was always dreaming and thinking odd things and could not herself remember any time when she had not been thinking things about grown-up people and the world they belonged to. She felt as if she had lived a long, long time.

At this moment she was remembering the voyage she had just made from Bombay with her father, Captain Crewe. She was thinking of the big ship, of the Lascars passing silently to and fro on it, of the children playing about on the hot deck, and of some young officers' wives who used to try to make her talk to them and laugh at the things she said.

Principally, she was thinking of what a queer thing it was that at one time one was in India in the blazing sun, and then in the middle of the ocean, and then driving in a strange vehicle through strange streets where the day was as dark as the night. She found this so puzzling that she moved closer to her father.

Go to the next page.

"Papa," she said in a low, mysterious little voice which was almost a whisper, "papa."

"What is it, darling?" Captain Crewe answered, holding her closer and looking down into her face. "What is Sara thinking of?"

"Is this the place?" Sara whispered, cuddling still closer to him. "Is it, papa?"

"Yes, little Sara, it is. We have reached it at last." And though she was only seven years old, she knew that he felt sad when he said it.

It seemed to her many years since he had begun to prepare her mind for "the place," as she always called it. Her mother had died when she was born, so she had never known or missed her. Her young, handsome, rich, petting father seemed to be the only relation she had in the world. They had always played together and been fond of each other. She only knew he was rich because she had heard people say so when they thought she was not listening, and she had also heard them say that when she grew up she would be rich, too. She did not know all that being rich meant. She had always lived in a beautiful bungalow, and had been used to seeing many servants who made salaams to her and called her 'Missee Sahib,' and gave her her own way in everything. She had had toys and pets and an ayah who worshipped her, and she had gradually learned that people who were rich had these things. That, however, was all she knew about it.

During her short life only one thing had troubled her, and that thing was 'the place' she was to be taken to some day. The climate of India was very bad for children, and as soon as possible they were sent away from it – generally to England and to school. She had seen other children go away, and had heard their fathers and mothers talk about the letters they received from them. She had known that she would be obliged to go also, and though sometimes her father's stories of the voyage and the new country had attracted her, she had been troubled by the thought that he could not stay with her.

Extract from: **A Little Princess** by Frances Hodgson Burnett

① How does the author describe Sara Crewe?

A   An odd-looking little girl of seven who looked much older

B   An older girl and very pretty

C   A girl of twelve with big eyes

D   A small girl with a large face

E   An ordinary schoolgirl

② Which word is similar in meaning to 'thoroughfares'?

A   Woodlands

B   Parklands

C   Streets

D   Shopping centres

E   Corridors

③ Where had the little girl travelled from?

A   London

B   France

C   Europe

D   England

E   Bombay

④ What was Sara always thinking about?

A   Other children

B   Older girls

C   Older boys

D   Grown-ups

E   Her father

⑤ What type of language device is used in the phrase 'the day was as dark as the night'?

A   Metaphor

B   Simile

C   Pronoun

D   Question

E   Verb

Go to the next page.

6   How did Sara feel when she saw the strange streets and the darkness of the daytime?

    A   She found them mysterious

    B   She found them enchanting

    C   She found them dangerous

    D   She found them enjoyable

    E   She found them puzzling

7   Why did Sara speak in a 'low, mysterious little voice'?

    A   She was happy

    B   She was feeling sick

    C   She was rather anxious

    D   She was enjoying everything

    E   She had a cold

8   Why did Sara's father hold her closer?

    A   He thought she was cold

    B   He thought she was poorly

    C   He was cold himself

    D   He was trying to reassure her

    E   He thought she might fall off the seat

9   What had happened to Sara's mother?

    A   She had stayed at home

    B   She had died

    C   She was waiting for her

    D   She had left them

    E   She was working

10   What did Sara think of her father?

    A   She hated him

    B   She was very fond of him

    C   She thought he was old

    D   She thought he was poor

    E   She thought he was very busy

Comprehension Test 8

 You have 8 minutes to complete the following exercise.
You have 10 questions to complete within the time given.

Read the passage and answer the questions that follow.

Mr Badger

THEY waited patiently for what seemed a very long time, stamping in the snow to keep their feet warm. At last they heard the sound of slow shuffling footsteps approaching the door from the inside. It seemed, as the Mole remarked to the Rat, like someone walking in carpet slippers that were too large for him and down at heel; which was intelligent of Mole, because that was exactly what it was.

There was the noise of a bolt shot back, and the door opened a few inches, enough to show a long snout and a pair of sleepy blinking eyes.

"Now, the VERY next time this happens," said a gruff and suspicious voice, "I shall be exceedingly angry. Who is it THIS time, disturbing people on such a night? Speak up!"

"Oh, Badger," cried the Rat, "let us in, please. It's me, Rat, and my friend Mole, and we've lost our way in the snow."

"What, Ratty, my dear little man!" exclaimed the Badger, in quite a different voice. "Come along in, both of you, at once. Why, you must be perished. Well I never! Lost in the snow! And in the Wild Wood, too, and at this time of night! But come in with you."

The two animals tumbled over each other in their eagerness to get inside, and heard the door shut behind them with great joy and relief.

The Badger, who wore a long dressing-gown, and whose slippers were indeed very down at heel, carried a flat candlestick in his paw and had probably been on his way to bed when their summons sounded. He looked kindly down on them and patted both their heads. "This is not the sort of night for small animals to be out," he said paternally. "I'm afraid you've been up to some of your pranks again, Ratty. But come along; come into the kitchen. There's a first-rate fire there, and supper and everything."

He shuffled on in front of them, carrying the light, and they followed him, nudging each other in an anticipating sort of way, down a long, gloomy, and, to tell the truth, decidedly shabby passage, into a sort of a central hall; out of which they could dimly see other long tunnel-like passages branching, passages mysterious and without apparent end. But there were doors in the hall as well — stout oaken comfortable-looking doors. One of these the Badger flung open, and at once they found themselves in all the glow and warmth of a large fire-lit kitchen.

Go to the next page.

The floor was well-worn red brick, and on the wide hearth burnt a fire of logs, between two attractive chimney-corners tucked away in the wall, well out of any suspicion of draught.
A couple of high-backed settles, facing each other on either side of the fire, gave further sitting accommodations for the sociably disposed. In the middle of the room stood a long table of plain boards placed on trestles, with benches down each side. At one end of it, where an arm-chair stood pushed back, were spread the remains of the Badger's plain but ample supper. Rows of spotless plates winked from the shelves of the dresser at the far end of the room, and from the rafters overhead hung hams, bundles of dried herbs, nets of onions, and baskets of eggs.

Extract from: **The Wind in the Willows** by Kenneth Grahame

1. What type of word is 'patiently'?

   A   Noun

   B   Pronoun

   C   Adverb

   D   Adjective

   E   Clause

2. What could be seen when the door opened a few inches?

   A   Two eyes and two feet

   B   A snout and sleepy eyes

   C   Two ears and two paws

   D   Two eyes and a tongue

   E   A tail and two paws

3. Which word is similar in meaning to 'gruff'?

   A   Hoarse

   B   Soft

   C   Kindly

   D   Gentle

   E   Loud

4. Why was Badger angry when they knocked on the door?

   A   He had been eating his tea

   B   He had probably been on his way to bed

   C   He had been washing his clothes

   D   He had been in the bath

   E   He was scared

(5) What phrase best describes Badger's slippers?

A   They were smart and checked

B   They were full of holes

C   They matched his dressing-gown

D   They were worn down on the heels

E   They were fluffy and pink

(6) How did Badger react when he saw his friends?

A   He was annoyed and angry

B   He was afraid and wanted them to go

C   He was pleased to see them

D   He was cross that they had come so late

E   He didn't want to share his tea

(7) Which phrase best describes Badger's kitchen?

A   It was large and empty

B   It was dark and gloomy

C   It was tunnel-like

D   It was mysterious and strange

E   It was warm and lit by the fire

(8) What hung from the rafters of the kitchen?

A   Dusty cobwebs

B   Christmas baubles

C   Bundles of newspapers

D   Bundles of dried herbs, hams, onions and eggs

E   Jampots and pans

(9) What sort of seating was there in the kitchen?

A   Stools and cushions

B   Benches and an arm-chair

C   Settles, benches and an arm-chair

D   Lots of comfy arm-chairs

E   A rocking chair

(10) In the context of the passage which word is similar in meaning to 'rows'?

A   Arguments

B   Lines

C   Squabbles

D   Prizes

E   Agreements

Comprehension Test 9

 You have 8 minutes to complete the following exercise.
You have 10 questions to complete within the time given.

Read the passage and answer the questions that follow.

Cyclone

Dorothy lived in the midst of the great Kansas prairies, with Uncle Henry, who was a farmer, and Aunt Em, who was the farmer's wife. Their house was small, for the lumber to build it had to be carried by wagon many miles. There were four walls, a floor and a roof, which made one room; and this room contained a rusty looking cookstove, a cupboard for the dishes, a table, three or four chairs, and the beds. Uncle Henry and Aunt Em had a big bed in one corner, and Dorothy a little bed in another corner. There was no garret at all, and no cellar – except a small hole dug in the ground, called a cyclone cellar, where the family could go in case one of those great whirlwinds arose, mighty enough to crush any building in its path. It was reached by a trap door in the middle of the floor, from which a ladder led down into the small, dark hole.

When Dorothy stood in the doorway and looked around, she could see nothing but the great grey prairie on every side. Not a tree nor a house broke the broad sweep of flat country that reached to the edge of the sky in all directions. The sun had baked the ploughed land into a grey mass, with little cracks running through it. Even the grass was not green, for the sun had burned the tops of the long blades until they were the same grey colour to be seen everywhere. Once, the house had been painted, but the sun blistered the paint and the rains washed it away, and now the house was as dull and grey as everything else.

When Aunt Em came there to live she was a young, pretty wife. The sun and wind had changed her, too. They had taken the sparkle from her eyes and left them a sober grey; they had taken the red from her cheeks and lips, and they were grey also. She was thin and gaunt, and never smiled now. When Dorothy, who was an orphan, first came to her, Aunt Em had been so startled by the child's laughter that she would scream and press her hand upon her heart whenever Dorothy's merry voice reached her ears; and she still looked at the little girl with wonder that she could find anything to laugh at.

Uncle Henry never laughed. He worked hard from morning till night and did not know what joy was. He was grey also, from his long beard to his rough boots, and he looked stern and solemn, and rarely spoke.

It was Toto that made Dorothy laugh and saved her from growing as grey as her other surroundings. Toto was not grey; he was a little black dog, with long silky hair and small black eyes that twinkled merrily on either side of his funny, wee nose. Toto played all day long, and Dorothy played with him, and loved him dearly.

Today, however, they were not playing. Uncle Henry sat upon the doorstep and looked anxiously at the sky, which was even grayer than usual. Dorothy stood in the door with Toto in her arms, and looked at the sky too. Aunt Em was washing the dishes.

From the far north they heard a low wail of the wind, and Uncle Henry and Dorothy could see where the long grass bowed in waves before the coming storm. There now came a sharp whistling in the air from the south, and as they turned their eyes that way they saw ripples in the grass coming from that direction also.

Suddenly Uncle Henry stood up.

"There's a cyclone coming, Em," he called to his wife. "I'll go look after the stock." Then he ran toward the sheds where the cows and horses were kept.

Aunt Em dropped her work and came to the door. One glance told her of the danger close at hand.

"Quick, Dorothy!" she screamed. "Run for the cellar!"

Toto jumped out of Dorothy's arms and hid under the bed, and the girl started to get him. Aunt Em, badly frightened, threw open the trap door in the floor and climbed down the ladder into the small, dark hole. Dorothy caught Toto at last and started to follow her aunt. When she was halfway across the room there came a great shriek from the wind, and the house shook so hard that she lost her footing and sat down suddenly upon the floor.

Then a strange thing happened.

The house whirled around two or three times and rose slowly through the air.

Extract from: **The Wonderful Wizard of Oz** by L. Frank Baum

Go to the next page.

1. What type of word is 'lumber'?

   A   Metaphor

   B   Simile

   C   Verb

   D   Noun

   E   Pronoun

2. Which word is similar in meaning to 'cellar'?

   A   Basement

   B   Loft

   C   Attic

   D   Tunnel

   E   Tomb

3. What type of word is 'arose'?

   A   Verb

   B   Adjective

   C   Adverb

   D   Noun

   E   Pronoun

4. What does the author mean by the country 'reached to the edge of the sky'?

   A   The land was hilly

   B   The sky was big

   C   It was a stormy sky

   D   The land was flat and merged with the sky

   E   There were fields

5. What does the author mean when he writes that 'the sun had baked the ploughed land'?

   A   The wind blew hard and made a loud noise

   B   The sun made her feel warm

   C   The sun made the land hard

   D   The sun was weak

   E   The sun didn't shine

6 What was Aunt Em like when she first came to live there?

A   She didn't eat her tea

B   She had a sparkle in her eyes

C   She was ill and grey

D   She was thin and gaunt

E   She was an orphan

7 What surprised Aunt Em?

A   The wind

B   Dorothy's laughter

C   Toto

D   Uncle Henry

E   The weather

8 What type of person was Uncle Henry?

A   Jolly

B   Mean

C   Noisy

D   Quiet

E   Merry

9 What type of word is 'merrily' in the fifth paragraph?

A   Adverb

B   Pronoun

C   Adjective

D   Clause

E   Noun

10 What stopped Dorothy growing as grey as her surroundings?

A   The weather

B   Living in the middle of a prairie

C   Uncle Henry

D   Aunt Em

E   Toto

Comprehension Test 10

 You have 8 minutes to complete the following exercise.
You have 10 questions to complete within the time given.

Read the poem and answer the questions that follow.

Macavity

Macavity's a Mystery Cat: he's called the Hidden Paw –
For he's the master criminal who can defy the Law.
He's the bafflement of Scotland Yard, the Flying Squad's despair:
For when they reach the scene of crime – Macavity's not there!

Macavity, Macavity, there's no one like Macavity,
He's broken every human law, he breaks the law of gravity.
His powers of levitation would make a fakir stare,
And when you reach the scene of crime – Macavity's not there!
You may seek him in the basement, you may look up in the air –
But I tell you once and once again, Macavity's not there!

Macavity's a ginger cat, he's very tall and thin;
You would know him if you saw him, for his eyes are sunken in.
His brow is deeply lined with thought, his head is highly domed;
His coat is dusty from neglect, his whiskers are uncombed.
He sways his head from side to side, with movements like a snake;
And when you think he's half asleep, he's always wide awake.

Macavity, Macavity, there's no one like Macavity,
For he's a fiend in feline shape, a monster of depravity.
You may meet him in a by-street, you may see him in the square –
But when a crime's discovered, then Macavity's not there!

He's outwardly respectable. (They say he cheats at cards.)
And his footprints are not found in any file of Scotland Yard's.
And when the larder's looted, or the jewel-case is rifled,
Or when the milk is missing, or another Peke's been stifled,
Or the greenhouse glass is broken, and the trellis past repair –
Ay, there's the wonder of the thing! Macavity's not there!

And when the Foreign Office find a Treaty's gone astray,
Or the Admiralty lose some plans and drawings by the way,
There may be a scrap of paper in the hall or on the stair –
But it's useless to investigate – Macavity's not there!

And when the loss has been disclosed, the Secret Service say:
"It must have been Macavity!" – but he's a mile away.
You'll be sure to find him resting, or a-licking of his thumbs,
Or engaged in doing complicated long division sums.

Macavity, Macavity, there's no one like Macavity,
There never was a Cat of such deceitfulness and suavity.
He always has an alibi, and one or two to spare:
At whatever time the deed took place – MACAVITY WASN'T THERE!
And they say that all the Cats whose wicked deeds are widely known
(I might mention Mungojerrie, I might mention Griddlebone)
Are nothing more than agents for the Cat who all the time
Just controls their operations: the Napoleon of Crime!

Poem by T.S. Eliot

① Which word is similar in meaning to 'bafflement'?

A   Anger

B   Annoyance

C   Bewilderment

D   Fright

E   Excitement

② What type of word is 'basement'?

A   Noun

B   Adverb

C   Adjective

D   Verb

E   Pronoun

③ What does the poet mean by 'his coat is dusty from neglect'?

A   He has a new coat

B   His fur is dirty because he doesn't clean it

C   He never wears a coat

D   He likes to dust in his coat

E   He forgets to take his coat off

④ What type of language device is the phrase 'with movements like a snake'?

A   Alliteration

B   Metaphor

C   Declarative

D   Simile

E   Question

Go to the next page.

(5) Which phrase is similar to the words 'a fiend in feline shape'?

A   A demon that looks like a cat

B   A cat thief

C   A monster cat

D   A friendly cat

E   A cat that looks like a friend

(6) Where are his footprints found?

A   In the larder

B   In the jewel-case

C   On the table

D   They are not found at all

E   In the file of Scotland Yard

(7) Why is it useless to investigate Macavity?

A   He is never there

B   He is in the basement

C   He pretends he is a snake

D   He is always asleep

E   He hides in the street

(8) What is Macavity likely to be doing by the time the Secret Service realise he is probably the thief?

A   He will be chasing mice

B   He will be sitting on a wall

C   He will be eating his dinner

D   He will be writing a letter

E   He will be doing long division sums

(9) Which word is opposite in meaning to 'complicated'?

A   Difficult

B   Simple

C   Intricate

D   Division

E   Useless

(10) Which phrase best describes an 'alibi'?

A   A washing basket

B   A type of confectionery

C   A fish supper

D   A reason to avoid blame

E   Being at the cinema

Comprehension Test 11

 You have 8 minutes to complete the following exercise.
You have 10 questions to complete within the time given.

Read the passage and answer the questions that follow.

Dickon

The sun shone down for nearly a week on the secret garden. The Secret Garden was what Mary called it when she was thinking of it. She liked the name, and she liked still more the feeling that when its beautiful old walls shut her in no one knew where she was. It seemed almost like being shut out of the world in some fairy place. The few books she had read and liked had been fairy-story books, and she had read of secret gardens in some of the stories. Sometimes people went to sleep in them for a hundred years, which she had thought must be rather stupid. She had no intention of going to sleep, and, in fact, she was becoming wider awake every day which passed at Misselthwaite. She was beginning to like to be out of doors; she no longer hated the wind, but enjoyed it. She could run faster, and longer, and she could skip up to a hundred. The bulbs in the secret garden must have been much astonished. Such nice clear places were made round them that they had all the breathing space they wanted, and really, if Mistress Mary had known it, they began to cheer up under the dark earth and work tremendously. The sun could get at them and warm them, and when the rain came down it could reach them at once, so they began to feel very much alive.

Mary was an odd, determined little person, and now she had something interesting to be determined about, she was very much absorbed indeed. She worked and dug and pulled up weeds steadily, only becoming more pleased with her work every hour instead of tiring of it. It seemed to her like a fascinating sort of play. She found many more of the sprouting pale green points than she had ever hoped to find. They seemed to be starting up everywhere and each day she was sure she found tiny new ones, some so tiny that they barely peeped above the earth. There were so many that she remembered what Martha had said about the "snowdrops by the thousands," and about bulbs spreading and making new ones. These had been left to themselves for ten years and perhaps they had spread, like the snowdrops, into thousands. She wondered how long it would be before they showed that they were flowers. Sometimes she stopped digging to look at the garden and try to imagine what it would be like when it was covered with thousands of lovely things in bloom.

Go to the next page.

During that week of sunshine, she became more intimate with Ben Weatherstaff. She surprised him several times by seeming to start up beside him as if she sprang out of the earth. The truth was that she was afraid that he would pick up his tools and go away if he saw her coming, so she always walked toward him as silently as possible. But, in fact, he did not object to her as strongly as he had at first. Perhaps he was secretly rather flattered by her evident desire for his elderly company. Then, also, she was more civil than she had been. He did not know that when she first saw him she spoke to him as she would have spoken to a native, and had not known that a cross, sturdy old Yorkshire man was not accustomed to salaam to his masters, and be merely commanded by them to do things.

He very seldom talked much and sometimes did not even answer Mary's questions except by a grunt, but this morning he said more than usual.

Extract from: **The Secret Garden** by Frances Hodgson Burnett

---

① Why did Mary like the name 'The Secret Garden'?

   A   It gave her the feeling no one knew where she was

   B   It felt as if it had been there a hundred years

   C   She liked gardening

   D   She liked sleeping there

   E   She read books there

② What were the bulbs in the garden doing?

   A   They were wet

   B   They were dead

   C   They were hiding

   D   They were breathing

   E   They were beginning to grow

③ How does the author describe Mary?

   A   Slow and dull

   B   A good girl

   C   An oddly determined child

   D   Always lazy and distracted

   E   Sometimes unhappy and morose

④ Which word is similar in meaning to 'absorbed'?

   A   Distracted

   B   Angry

   C   Engrossed

   D   Frustrated

   E   Hardworking

5 Which word is similar in meaning to 'sprouting'?

A Growing

B Dying

C Lifting

D Pushing

E Flattening

6 What had Martha told her about bulbs?

A That they often died

B That they liked the dark

C That you planted them every year

D That they spread and made new ones

E That they loved the sun

7 What did Mary do when she stopped digging?

A She thought of dinner

B She looked at the sky

C She played with the toys

D She tried to imagine the flowers

E She looked at the birds

8 What is meant by the phrase 'things in bloom'?

A Trees without leaves

B The plants blowing in the wind

C The garden full of toys

D All the plants in flower

E The tools in the toolbox

9 What did Mary do that surprised Ben Weatherstaff?

A She said boo

B She jumped out at him

C She popped up behind a wall

D She shouted to him

E She approached him as quietly as possible

10 What was Mary afraid Ben Weatherstaff would do if he saw her coming?

A He would ask her to leave the garden

B He would ask her to water the bulbs

C He would go away

D He would have lunch

E He would bury the gardening tools

Comprehension Test 12

 You have 8 minutes to complete the following exercise.
You have 10 questions to complete within the time given.

Read the passage and answer the questions that follow.

The Old House

Long forgotten, down a lonely lane, through an avenue of tall elms which formed a green tunnel, stood an abandoned house. Once upon a time the house had stood proud and smart amongst well-kept gardens and orchards.

The family who had once laughed, chatted and sung within its walls had gone. Children no longer climbed the trees or made dens around the gardens. It had been home to a wealthy family who had enjoyed living and working at the homestead. All that could be seen from the windows of the house had belonged to them and they had enjoyed the seasons and the nature within the meadows.

The old house had been abandoned in days gone by. The wild overgrown gardens spoke of lives once lived, with its small orchard and skeleton frame of a greenhouse, now enmeshed in brambles and rosebay willowherb. The vegetable garden, once the pride of the owner, now lay underneath a mat of chickweed and ivy. Only the apple trees still produced juicy red apples as they once did, though the ground was thick with rotting fallen fruit in the absence of hands to pick them, wash them and place them carefully in the fruit bowl.

The roof had fallen in at one end and the stone slates lay on the ground like a pack of fallen playing cards. Moss streaked the walls, making no distinction between the inside and the outside, and the windows and doors, like gaping mouths, moaned softly in the moorland wind. The chimney still stood proud and tall like a sentinel watching the comings and goings of the creatures who now inhabited the deserted dwelling.

On stormy nights when the rain lashed the stonework, things would move. The old door hanging by its hinges creaked backwards and forwards. Felting on the roof where the tiles once were flapped like flags and the movement of animals in every part of the structure would, from time to time, make plaster, stone and cement tumble down and shatter onto the flagged floor.

The passer-by might look and shiver, thinking of the families that had gone, of the abandonment, of the emptiness, and their lingering impression would be one of sadness. But that was not the case at all. The old house was full of life, full of the scurry of small creatures, teeming with insect worlds. Its rafters sheltered birds and bats and the waft of wings shook the spiders' webs which hung like lace curtains across the roof span. Night owls rested in the recesses of the roof beams, still as statues, listening with intent, and wily old fox families crept stealthily around the perimeter sniffing out that evening's meal. Under piles of leaves wafted into the corners of the rooms snuggled the spiky hedgehog inhabitants and old Brock the badger with his nose to the ground, his humbug striped head glimmering in the moonlight.

Families of fluffy brown rabbits leaped and loped around the rooms, nibbling the dandelions which grew in the dining room. In the cellars, under the house, slithering slow-worms celebrated the dampness and frogs revelled in the water that seeped up from the ground. A clamour of rooks shouted commands from the very top of the chimney, swooping amongst the ruins like black shadows.

The old house was full, more than full, bursting and overflowing with life as never before. Now home to a multitude, not just a few.

Indeed every nook and cranny of the old house now served as a cosy home for creatures. Where once the owner of the house would have swept away the earwigs from the hallway, they were now lodged safely under every loose tile. Where the net curtains had prevented the night-time moths from entering the bedrooms, these creatures now flew freely though the uninterrupted spaces.

(1) Which phrase best describes the garden?

A   Manicured and well laid out

B   A cottage garden

C   A vegetable patch

D   An allotment

E   Neglected and wild

(2) Which word is similar in meaning to 'enmeshed'?

A   Concealed

B   Curved

C   Entangled

D   Behind

E   Escaped

(3) What type of language device is 'the stone slates lay on the ground like a pack of fallen playing cards?'

A   Metaphor

B   Conjunction

C   Alliteration

D   Simile

E   Verb

(4) Which word is similar in meaning to 'distinction'?

A   Notification

B   Departure

C   Determination

D   Difference

E   Objection

Go to the next page.

5 Why was the empty house full of life?

A   People held parties there

B   Ghosts lived in the rooms

C   Many creatures inhabited the rooms

D   Workmen were repairing it

E   It was student accommodation

6 What type of language device is 'the waft of wings'?

A   Metaphor

B   Simile

C   Conjunction

D   Verb

E   Alliteration

7 Which creatures inhabited the roof?

A   Slow-worms

B   Cats

C   Spiders

D   Rooks

E   Rabbits

8 Which phrase is similar in meaning to 'recess'?

A   An indentation in a wall

B   An opening to the outside

C   A loft

D   An attic

E   A cellar

9 Why did the author write the phrase 'slow-worms celebrated the dampness'?

A   Because slow-worms are horrible things

B   Because slow-worms like having parties

C   Because slow-worms live in soil

D   Because slow-worms like to live in the damp and the dark

E   Because slow-worms are very wriggly

10 Which word is similar in meaning to 'multitude'?

A   Multipack

B   Crowd

C   Monster

D   Moth

E   Undergrowth

Comprehension Test 13

 You have 8 minutes to complete the following exercise.
You have 10 questions to complete within the time given.

Read the passage and answer the questions that follow.

Water Babies

Once upon a time there was a little chimney-sweep, and his name was Tom. That is a short name, and you have heard it before, so you will not have much trouble in remembering it. He lived in a great town in the North country, where there were plenty of chimneys to sweep, and plenty of money for Tom to earn and his master to spend. He could not read nor write, and did not care to do either; and he never washed himself, for there was no water up the court where he lived. He had never been taught to say his prayers. He never had heard of God, or of Christ, except in words which you never have heard, and which it would have been well if he had never heard. He cried half his time, and laughed the other half. He cried when he had to climb the dark flues, rubbing his poor knees and elbows raw; and when the soot got into his eyes, which it did every day in the week; and when his master beat him, which he did every day in the week; and when he had not enough to eat, which happened every day in the week likewise. And he laughed the other half of the day, when he was tossing halfpennies with the other boys, or playing leap-frog over the posts, or bowling stones at the horses' legs as they trotted by, which last was excellent fun, when there was a wall at hand behind which to hide. As for chimney-sweeping, and being hungry, and being beaten, he took all that for the way of the world, like the rain and snow and thunder, and stood manfully with his back to it till it was over, as his old donkey did to a hail-storm; and then shook his ears and was as jolly as ever; and thought of the fine times coming, when he would be a man, and a master sweep, and sit in the public-house with a quart of beer and a long pipe, and play cards for silver money, and wear velveteens and ankle-jacks, and keep a white bull-dog with one grey ear, and carry her puppies in his pocket, just like a man. And he would have apprentices, one, two, three, if he could. How he would bully them, and knock them about, just as his master did to him; and make them carry home the soot sacks, while he rode before them on his donkey, with a pipe in his mouth and a flower in his button-hole, like a king at the head of his army. Yes, there were good times coming; and, when his master let him have a pull at the leavings of his beer, Tom was the jolliest boy in the whole town.

One day a smart little groom rode into the court where Tom lived. Tom was just hiding behind a wall, to heave half a brick at his horse's legs, as is the custom of that country when they welcome

Go to the next page.

strangers; but the groom saw him, and halloed to him to know where Mr. Grimes, the chimney-sweep, lived. Now, Mr. Grimes was Tom's own master, and Tom was a good man of business, and always civil to customers, so he put the half-brick down quietly behind the wall, and proceeded to take orders.

Mr. Grimes was to come up next morning to Sir John Harthover's, at the Place, for his old chimney-sweep was gone to prison, and the chimneys wanted sweeping. And so he rode away, not giving Tom time to ask what the sweep had gone to prison for, which was a matter of interest to Tom, as he had been in prison once or twice himself. Moreover, the groom looked so very neat and clean, with his drab gaiters, drab breeches, drab jacket, snow-white tie with a smart pin in it, and clean round ruddy face, that Tom was offended and disgusted at his appearance, and considered him a stuck-up fellow, who gave himself airs because he wore smart clothes, and other people paid for them; and went behind the wall to fetch the half-brick after all; but did not, remembering that he had come in the way of business, and was, as it were, under a flag of truce.

Extract from: **The Water Babies** by Charles Kingsley

---

1. Where did Tom live?
   A In the South
   B In London
   C In the North country
   D In Spain
   E In Scotland

2. What did Tom have to do each day of the week?
   A Pray to God
   B Climb up chimneys
   C Read and write
   D Play games
   E Mind his own business

3. What made Tom feel happy?
   A Digging in the snow
   B Riding horses
   C Reading and writing
   D Playing with his friends
   E Saying his prayers

4. Which word is similar in meaning to 'manfully'?
   A Bravely
   B Cowardly
   C Frightened
   D Subdued
   E Faithfully

5 What did Tom want to be when he grew up?

A   A dog trainer

B   The owner of a public-house

C   A shopkeeper

D   A coal miner

E   A master chimney-sweep

6 What type of language device is the phrase 'like a king at the head of his army'?

A   Metaphor

B   Simile

C   Alliteration

D   Question

E   Verb

7 What does the author mean by the phrase 'Tom was a good man of business, and always civil to customers'?

A   Tom hated the customers

B   Tom was a good businessman but hated the customers

C   Tom was always rude to the customers

D   Tom was a good businessman and always polite to the customers

E   Tom enjoyed doing business but not with the customers

8 What type of word is 'ruddy'?

A   Noun

B   Adjective

C   Pronoun

D   Adverb

E   Question

9 How did Tom feel about the smart appearance of the groom?

A   It disgusted him

B   He thought the groom looked lovely

C   The sight of the groom upset him

D   He felt very scruffy in comparison

E   He decided to buy new clothes

10 What is the meaning of the word 'truce'?

A   To fly a flag three times

B   To start fighting

C   To suspend fighting

D   To start flying a flag

E   To raise a flagpole

Comprehension Test 14

 You have 8 minutes to complete the following exercise.
You have 10 questions to complete within the time given.

Read the passage and answer the questions that follow.

Digging for Treasure

Well, when we had agreed to dig for treasure we all went down into the cellar and lighted the gas. Oswald would have liked to dig there, but it is stone flags. We looked among the old boxes and broken chairs and fenders and empty bottles and things, and at last we found the spades we had to dig in the sand with when we went to the seaside three years ago. They are not silly, babyish, wooden spades, that split if you look at them, but good iron, with a blue mark across the top of the iron part, and yellow wooden handles. We wasted a little time getting them dusted, because the girls wouldn't dig with spades that had cobwebs on them. Girls would never do for African explorers or anything like that, they are too beastly particular.

It was no use doing the thing by halves. We marked out a sort of square in the mouldy part of the garden, about three yards across, and began to dig. But we found nothing except worms and stones – and the ground was very hard.

So we thought we'd try another part of the garden, and we found a place in the big round flower bed, where the ground was much softer. We thought we'd make a smaller hole to begin with, and it was much better. We dug and dug and dug, and it was jolly hard work! We got very hot digging, but we found nothing.

Presently Albert-next-door looked over the wall. We do not like him very much, but we let him play with us sometimes, because his father is dead, and you must not be unkind to orphans, even if their mothers are alive. Albert is always very tidy. He wears frilly collars and velvet knickerbockers. I can't think how he can bear to.

So we said, "Hallo!"

And he said, "What are you up to?"

"We're digging for treasure," said Alice; "an ancient parchment revealed to us the place of concealment. Come over and help us. When we have dug deep enough we shall find a great pot of red clay, full of gold and precious jewels."

Albert-next-door only sniggered and said, "What silly nonsense!" He cannot play properly at all. It is very strange, because he has a very nice uncle. You see, Albert-next-door doesn't care for reading, and he has not read nearly so many books as we have, so he is very foolish and ignorant, but it cannot be helped, and you just have to put up with it when you want him to do anything. Besides, it is wrong to be angry with people for not being so clever as you are yourself. It is not always their faults.

So Oswald said, "Come and dig! Then you shall share the treasure when we've found it."

But he said, "I shan't – I don't like digging – and I'm just going in to my tea."

"Come along and dig, there's a good boy," Alice said. "You can use my spade. It's much the best –"

So he came along and dug, and when once he was over the wall we kept him at it, and we worked as well, of course, and the hole got deep. Pincher worked too – he is our dog and he is very good at digging. He digs for rats in the dustbin sometimes, and gets very dirty. But we love our dog, even when his face wants washing.

"I expect we shall have to make a tunnel," Oswald said, "to reach the rich treasure." So he jumped into the hole and began to dig at one side. After that we took it in turns to dig at the tunnel, and Pincher was most useful in scraping the earth out of the tunnel – he does it with his back feet when you say "Rats!" and he digs with his front ones, and burrows with his nose as well.

Extract from: *The Story of the Treasure Seekers* by Edith Nesbit

Go to the next page.

1. What were they digging for?

   A   Weeds

   B   Treasure

   C   Onions

   D   Dog bones

   E   Stones

2. What did they have to do to the spades before the girls would dig with them?

   A   Dust them

   B   Try them out

   C   Paint them

   D   Swap them

   E   Get the right size

3. Why was it that girls 'would never do for African explorers'?

   A   They would rather explore India

   B   They were too sensible

   C   They were far too particular

   D   They didn't like animals

   E   They were too clever

4. How did Albert know they were digging?

   A   He looked out of the window

   B   He looked through the fence

   C   He looked through binoculars

   D   He looked over the wall

   E   His mother told him

5. What type of word is 'frilly'?

   A   Adverb

   B   Verb

   C   Pronoun

   D   Noun

   E   Adjective

(6) Which word is similar in meaning to 'sniggered'?

A   Laughed

B   Grumbled

C   Muttered

D   Smirked

E   Joked

(7) What excuse did Albert give for not staying and digging?

A   He had to go to school

B   He didn't have a spade

C   He was scared of dogs

D   He didn't like cobwebs

E   He was going in for tea

(8) Who was Pincher?

A   Their friend

B   Their dog

C   Their pet rat

D   Their grandma

E   Albert's nickname

(9) What type of word is 'dustbin'?

A   Noun

B   Verb

C   Adjective

D   Pronoun

E   Clause

(10) What type of word is 'Pincher'?

A   Pronoun

B   Verb

C   Proper noun

D   Adjective

E   Collective noun

Comprehension Test 15

 You have 10 minutes to complete the following exercise.
You have 10 questions to complete within the time given.

Read the article and answer the questions that follow.

The 440-million-year-old Scottish fungus which kick-started the human race

Some 440 million years ago this tiny organism was among the first to make its way out of the seas and begin colonising the land.

It is the oldest example of a land-dwelling species ever discovered in the fossil record. Only sea creatures have been found which are older.

But crucially for humans, this early pioneer kick-started the process of rot and soil formation which eventually allowed plants to flourish, tempting animals on to dry land.

Examples of the diminutive Tortotubus fungus – shorter than the width of a human hair – were discovered on the Scottish Inner Hebridean island of Kerrera, and in Gotland, Sweden by scientists from the University of Cambridge.

"During the period when this organism existed, life was almost entirely restricted to the oceans: nothing more complex than simple mossy and lichen-like plants had yet evolved on the land," said the paper's author Dr Martin Smith, who conducted the work while at the University of Cambridge's Department of Earth Sciences, and is now based at Durham University.

"But before there could be flowering plants or trees, or the animals that depend on them, the processes of rot and soil formation needed to be established."

Pinpointing when life first migrated from the seas to the land is tricky because fossilised examples of the earliest colonisers are rare. It is generally agreed that the transition started in the early Palaeozoic Era, between 500 and 450 million years ago.

Before any complex forms of life could live on land, there needed to be nutrients there to support them. Fungi played a key role in the move to land by beginning the rotting process, allowing a layer of fertile soil to build up, which enabled plants to establish root systems. In turn those plants were able to support animal life which would eventually lead to humans.

Early fungi like Tortotubus started the process by getting nitrogen and oxygen into the soil. Decomposing fungi convert nitrogen-containing compounds in plant and animal waste and remains back into nitrates, which are incorporated into the soil and can again be taken up by plants.

"What we see in this fossil is complex fungal 'behaviour' in some of the earliest terrestrial ecosystems – contributing to soil formation and kick-starting the process of rotting on land," added Dr Smith. A question, however, is what was there for Tortotubus to decompose?

"It's likely that there were bacteria or algae on land during this period, but these organisms are rarely found as fossils."

And the fungus may even have been able to form mushrooms, as it follows a similar pattern to today's organisms.

"This fossil provides a hint that mushroom-forming fungi may have colonised the land before the first animals left the oceans," added Dr Smith.

"It fills an important gap in the evolution of life on land."

In 2004 a fossilised millipede was discovered in Stonehaven, north-east Scotland, which is believed to be the oldest land animal ever found, dating from 420 million years ago.

Extract from: *The Telegraph 2nd March 2016* by Sarah Knapton, Science Editor

Go to the next page.

(1) How old was the fungus fossil?

A   40 000 years old

B   44 000 years old

C   440 000 000 years old

D   440 000 years old

E   404 000 years old

(2) Which phrase best describes the word 'colonise'?

A   To settle in a place

B   To fight an army

C   To enjoy living in a place

D   To conquer the country

E   To escape from a place

(3) What, in the passage, tempted animals on to dry land?

A   The sea became rough

B   The fungus formed soil

C   The animals grew legs

D   The animals preferred the land

E   The sea flooded the land

(4) How small is the Tortotubus fungus?

A   Smaller than a pea

B   Smaller than a finger

C   Smaller than a shrimp

D   Shorter than any other fungus

E   Shorter than the width of a human hair

(5) What type of word is 'fungus'?

A   Verb

B   Noun

C   Adjective

D   Preposition

E   Pronoun

6 Which word is similar in meaning to 'rotting'?

A   Messy

B   Flaky

C   Dirty

D   Decomposing

E   Pollution

7 Which phrase best describes the word 'fossil'?

A   A rock

B   An antique

C   A petrified impression

D   A clay mould

E   A rock ore

8 What type of creatures have been found that are older than the Tortotubus fungus?

A   Sea horses

B   Shells

C   Seaweed

D   Sea creatures

E   Shrimps

9 In which two places were the Tortotubus fungi discovered?

A   Scotland and England

B   England and America

C   Kerrera and Guernsey

D   England and Sweden

E   Sweden and Scotland

10 What type of word is 'entirely' in the phrase 'life was almost entirely restricted to the oceans'?

A   Adverb

B   Pronoun

C   Verb

D   Adjective

E   Synonym

Comprehension Test 16

INSTRUCTIONS

 You have 8 minutes to complete the following exercise.
You have 10 questions to complete within the time given.

Read the passage and answer the questions that follow.

Pirates

For over 300 years, we have thrilled to the antics of fictional and fictionalised pirates from Blackbeard to Jack Sparrow. Pirates have existed since the early seventeenth century.

The subject of pirates has been widely used by film-makers, one of the most well-known films being *Pirates of the Caribbean*, starring Johnny Depp as Jack Sparrow.

Pirates are featured in children's storybooks such as Captain Pugwash, the incompetent pirate, and Captain Hook from *Peter Pan*. An author called Robert Louis Stevenson wrote a book called *Treasure Island* and this produced the first popular images of a salty pirate wandering along on a wooden leg with a parrot on his shoulder, holding a treasure map. In *Peter Pan* the famous Captain Hook is a pirate with a hook instead of a hand (it had been bitten off by a crocodile!). Hook is forever bent on destroying Peter Pan with the help of his first mate, Mr Smee.

However, pirates are not just fictional characters and there are still pirates today, though very few and these tend to operate in the South China Sea.

Throughout history there have been people willing to rob others. Pirates robbed people at sea, targeting ships carrying goods between countries, though some pirates launched attacks on coastal towns.

Pirates in ancient times threatened the trading routes of ancient Greece, seizing cargoes of grain and olive oil from Roman ships. Some pirates travelled huge distances, such as the Vikings who travelled from Norway to England to plunder villages.

Blackbeard and his crew of pirates terrorised sailors on the Atlantic Ocean and Caribbean Sea from 1716 to 1718. In the dim light of dawn, when the pirate ships were hardly visible, they would approach and ambush ships carrying passengers and cargo.

When the pirates had spotted their victims' ship they would determine the ship's nationality by looking for the flag. They would then hoist the same flag on their ship, making them appear to be friendly. Now able to draw close to the unsuspecting ship, the pirates would hoist Blackbeard's flag at the last moment. Usually the crew of the victims' ship would surrender without a fight as soon as they saw Blackbeard's flag; if they didn't then a more vicious attack would take place.

The use of real pirates such as Blackbeard in fictional contexts and stories is common. For example, we have Blackbeard alongside the fictional Jack Sparrow in *Pirates of the Caribbean* and Blackbeard also turns up in the fictional tale *Treasure Island*.

When Christopher Columbus had established contact between Europe and the Caribbean Islands, large Spanish ships called galleons began to sail back and forth laden with precious cargoes such as gold, silver and gems. There were many pirate attacks and the galleons were forced to sail together in fleets with armed vessels for protection. As the islands began to be settled and new towns grew up, they too became victims of vicious attacks from pirates.

Many of the famous pirates had a terrifying reputation and they advertised this by flying gruesome flags, including the 'Jolly Roger' with its picture of a skull and crossbones. Flying the Jolly Roger instilled fear in whatever ship was being attacked so that they would surrender immediately. Merchant vessels were terrified of the pirates and rarely assumed that they could win a fight against them.

Thousands of pirates were active between 1650 and 1720 and these years are known as the 'Golden Age' of piracy.

Famous pirates from this period include Henry Morgan, William 'Captain Kidd', 'Calico Jack' Rackham, Bartholomew Roberts and the famous Blackbeard, whose real name was Edward Teach.

Go to the next page.

1. Which is a similar phrase to 'thrilled to the antics'?

   A   Scared of the ants

   B   Enjoyed the funfair

   C   Found pleasure in studying arts

   D   Enjoyed visiting aunties

   E   Found the activities very exciting

2. Which is a similar word to 'incompetent'?

   A   Courageous

   B   Continent

   C   Inept

   D   Disgraceful

   E   Evil

3. What type of word is 'surrender'?

   A   Proper noun

   B   Plural noun

   C   Verb

   D   Collective noun

   E   Adverb

4. What were the cargoes of the galleons?

   A   Tea and sugar

   B   Coffee and biscuits

   C   Herbs and spices

   D   Silver and gold

   E   Fruit and plants

5. For how many years did the 'Golden Age' of piracy last?

   A   Four years

   B   Two years

   C   Seventy-seven years

   D   Seventy years

   E   Eighty years

6 How did the galleons protect their precious cargoes?

A   They had camouflage

B   They sailed in fleets

C   They moved very quickly

D   They only sailed at night

E   They disguised themselves as pirate ships

7 How did the pirates show that they were fierce and nasty?

A   They were always making growling noises

B   They said "aha" very loudly

C   They flew flags with scary pictures on

D   They had scarves with skulls on them

E   They had hooks instead of hands

8 Which phrase is similar in meaning to 'Many of the famous pirates had a terrifying reputation'?

A   The pirates had a scary dog called reputation

B   The pirates were terrified of being caught

C   They had a very big sword

D   The pirates were known to be very frightening

E   They had a very large cannon

9 What was the 'Jolly Roger'?

A   A friendly pirate

B   A Spanish galleon

C   A type of cannon

D   A protection vessel

E   A flag with skull and crossbones on it

10 Where does piracy still exist today?

A   In the Antarctic Ocean

B   In Spain

C   In the South China Sea

D   In the Mediterranean Sea

E   In the English Channel

Comprehension Test 17

 INSTRUCTIONS

 You have 8 minutes to complete the following exercise.
You have 10 questions to complete within the time given.

Read the passage and answer the questions that follow.

Imagination

It was a cold grey day in early December. The wind blew in from the northeast bringing the icy sting of Nordic sleet.

The sound of the frozen rain like fistfuls of grit thrown at the windowpane. Although it was only just past two in the afternoon, the daylight had all but gone, obliterated by the glowering grey skies. What little light remained struggled to reach the far corners of the room.

I watched the curtains of snow slanting across the forests and fields, adding a new and fresh topping to crusts of old slush and ice. Gradually the skies grew darker. It was too early for nightfall – this was the snowstorm – and perhaps it would soon pass over. I wasn't fond of the dark; it made me nervous and unsettled and I wished I lived further south where the days and nights were more equal in length.

The pallor of winter in the far north closed in early. It shrouded the hills and peaks in a dismal monotony, broken only occasionally when, usually after a heavy snowfall, the lid of cloud would lift. The glorious sunlight would burst through, warming the fields with a blast of gold that ignited your spirits and sent you into the outdoors with a sled in tow.

But today it was dark, very dark, and I was alone in the house. I didn't like being alone; my imagination was the problem. It worked well, too well in fact, and it drew exclamation marks after every solitary sound, after every fleeting shadow or waft of air.

The creak of the old wooden bench broke the silence, sending a spike of fright through my body. It was just the fat old cat springing onto the seat, causing the pine wood to bend in response.

I took down a leatherbound book from the bookcase and decided to read in order to take my mind to another place rather than allowing it to imagine all manner of uncomfortable things. Reading would occupy my mind and give my overworked senses a rest.

The book was old, a present from the old lady next door. She had passed away earlier in the winter and had left me this book to remember her by. The title of the book was *Philosophy for a Happy Life* and I didn't really understand what that meant, but Mother said it was about a subject called philosophy which was the study of how the mind works. Well, my mind – the mind of an eleven year old boy – was certainly working, that's for sure.

Perhaps there might be something in the book to take my mind off the shadows in the corners, the creaking floorboards, the moaning wind and even my own heart beating.

Leathery and musty, the pages well thumbed, it smelt of her and her cottage and as I thought of her I began to scare myself, to feel fluttery with fear. Perhaps she was here; perhaps she lingered on. How silly, I thought – she was such a sweet person. She had lived alone for many years and she wasn't ever afraid. She said life was what you made it.

The book had stood on her shelf and she would take it down and read just a sentence to me but most of the time I didn't understand any of it. Then I saw the words on the open page: 'You make reality with your thoughts, and so be sure yours are happy ones.' I laughed out loud and as I lifted my head, I saw the snow beginning to ease and knew the sun would be lighting up the world once again.

1) What type of language is 'frozen rain like fistfuls of grit'?

A   Metaphor

B   Simile

C   Alliteration

D   Phrase

E   Clause

2) Which word is similar in meaning to 'obliterated'?

A   Opened

B   Allowed

C   Marked

D   Finished

E   Eliminated

3) How did the author feel about the arrival of the dark days of winter?

A   Surprised

B   Unhappy

C   Excited

D   Bored

E   Puzzled

4) What type of language is 'shrouded'?

A   Verb

B   Adjective

C   Adverb

D   Noun

E   Pronoun

Go to the next page.

(5) What does the author mean when he writes that his imagination 'drew exclamation marks'?

A   His imagination could write

B   His imagination made things seem very alarming

C   His imagination was poor

D   His imagination could have worked better

E   His imagination annoyed him

(6) What was the cause of the noise that scared the author?

A   The dog and its bone

B   The bench breaking

C   The bench falling over

D   The cat going out

E   The cat jumping on the bench

(7) What did the book smell of?

A   Fish and chips

B   Cats and fish

C   Cottage cheese

D   Leather and the neighbour

E   Dampness

(8) What did the book say about making reality?

A   You make it with actions

B   You make it with thoughts

C   You make it with a recipe

D   You make it with a book

E   You make it with a decision

(9) How did the author feel when reading the page?

A   Silly and depressed

B   Amused because it seemed to be true

C   The sentence was a lie

D   The sentence made him more scared

E   The sentence made him feel stupid and upset

(10) What phrase sums up the theme of the story?

A   Imagination is a curse

B   Imagination is helpful

C   Imagination is a nuisance

D   A good imagination is useful

E   Imagination can be a good thing or a bad thing

Comprehension Test 18

 You have 10 minutes to complete the following exercise. You have 10 questions to complete within the time given.

Read the passage and answer the questions that follow.

The Greenwich Time Ball

Long before the development of telegraphic, radio and microwave technologies to keep accurate time, 'time balls' – spherical devices that descended at the same time every day and were large enough to be spotted by ships miles away – were the global standard.

In Victorian times, the Thames was thronging with ships. The only way to know if your watch or clock was telling the correct time was to look towards the roof of the Greenwich Observatory.

On the deck of the many ships, officers would stand ready with their pocket watch in their hands waiting for the signal from Greenwich. On the top of the observatory sat the bright red time ball.

The ball rests on a metal spike and each day at 12:55 the time ball rises halfway up its mast. At 12:58 it rises all the way to the top. At 13:00 exactly the ball drops and so provides a signal to anyone looking. At this point the officers would check their watches. Of course if you were looking in the wrong direction you would have to wait until the next day before it happened again.

Time balls were one of the first significant attempts at building a global standard for keeping time. The ringing of church bells on the hour – popularised in fourteenth-century Europe – was wildly inaccurate. The development of chronometers in the eighteenth century enabled ships crossing oceans to keep reliable time on board, but international time remained difficult to track. In 1829, British Navy captain Robert Wauchope came up with a solution: a large ball dropped at an exact, specific time that could be seen for miles by approaching vessels. This would allow sailors to adjust their marine chronometers to be synchronised with the accurate time ball.

The time ball worked so well that Wauchope passed along his idea to his Royal Navy commanders and the US Navy. Four years later, a time ball was installed at the Royal Observatory in Greenwich, England, where it still falls at exactly 1 p.m. Greenwich Mean Time, signalling the time to the world.

In 1845, the US Naval Observatory in Washington, DC installed the first American time ball using a 'gum elastic composition' supplied by Charles Goodyear, the inventor of vulcanised rubber. The ball dropped every day at 12 noon Eastern Standard Time.

Go to the next page.

The Washington, DC time ball dropped every day for nine decades to set the time in the nation's capital. It was moved in 1885 to the State, War, and Navy Building (now the Eisenhower Executive Office Building). 'Ball time' was kept until 1936, when the device was officially retired after advances in telegraphic and radio technologies.

Although the time-ball device provided the seafaring population with accurate timekeeping, the majority of the British population did not have access to a clock. In the past only the richest people could afford to buy clocks and watches of their own and most people relied on public sundials to tell the time. This led to different local times across the country, with clocks on the eastern side of the country about 30 minutes ahead of those in the west. The difficulties created by everyone using their own local time eventually led to the creation of standard time based on the Prime Meridian at Greenwich.

In 1852 the Greenwich Observatory had its own official clock installed called the 'Shepherd Master Clock'. This was a clock for the public to use, not just for the sailors. It was connected to another clock fastened to the gates of the observatory and was the first clock to show Greenwich Mean Time directly to the public.

(1) Which word is similar in meaning to 'thronging'?

    A   Building

    B   Crowded

    C   Watering

    D   Moving

    E   Backing

(2) How could you check the correct time?

    A   Look towards the sun

    B   Look at the ship flags

    C   Look at your phone

    D   Look at the roof of the observatory

    E   Look at the stars

(3) What was on the top of the observatory?

    A   The roof

    B   A lot of chimneys

    C   A telescope

    D   A flagpole

    E   A bright red time ball

(4) What happens to the ball at 13:00?

    A   It's used for football

    B   It moves around

    C   It rises to the top of the mast

    D   It bounces up and down

    E   It falls down the mast

5 What would happen if you were looking the wrong way at 13:00?

    A   You would be late for an appointment

    B   You would be too early

    C   You would have to wait 24 hours before you could check the time again

    D   You would crash into the ship

    E   You would have to use your watch

6 How did ordinary people tell the time in Victorian times?

    A   They used public sundials

    B   They used the sun

    C   They used the planets

    D   They asked their neighbour

    E   They guessed

7 What problems arose from the use of sundials?

    A   There were a great deal of missed appointments

    B   There was a variation in time from east to west

    C   There wasn't a way of telling the time on rainy days

    D   There weren't a lot of sundials

    E   There wasn't a lot of sunshine

8 Which word is similar in meaning to 'installed'?

    A   Placed

    B   Mended

    C   Created

    D   Finished

    E   Ended

9 What happened in 1852?

    A   The ball fell off the roof

    B   The gates were fastened

    C   The observatory had a clock fixed to the gates

    D   The public were allowed to visit the observatory

    E   The ball was fixed to the gates

10 Where was the observatory situated?

    A   In Greenwich

    B   In a church

    C   On a ship

    D   In the East

    E   On an island in the Thames

Comprehension Test 19

 You have 8 minutes to complete the following exercise.
You have 10 questions to complete within the time given.

Read the passage and answer the questions that follow.

The Box

In the middle of the living room sat the box. Not just a box, more of a piece of furniture, thought Eliza as Mother rubbed a duster across the front panels.

"It's a blanket box," said Mother, "Aunt Charlotte has had this in her hallway since I can first remember." The four panels on the front of the box were deeply carved with a circular pattern, some like flowers, some more intricate than others. Eliza recognised that they were mandala symbols.

Eliza knew about the mandala symbol. Her great-grandfather had shown her this symbol on a creased brown money wallet that he carried with him in his waistcoat pocket. He would take it with them to buy sweeties at the corner shop and the shopkeeper had commented on the design.

Aadi the shopkeeper had arrived in England long ago. He had left his home in Hyderabad in India to make a new life in England. Life had been difficult there with first floods and then drought. His family had been very poor but had saved all the money they could so they could pay for the journey to England. Aadi's family wanted a better life for their son.

The mandala symbol was important to many Indians. Aadi had told her that it was a spiritual symbol used in Indian religions and the intricate interlocking circles represented the universe,

Earth, Sun and planets as well as the connectedness of friends and family. He went on to say that the mandala reminds us that we are all one spirit and so we are at home wherever we are.

"Why is the mandala carved on the blanket box?" Eliza asked her mother. "Aunt Charlotte hasn't come to England from India – she only came across the Irish Sea from Dublin."

Mother explained that Aunt Charlotte had come to England as a young girl, with her mother, after many members of the family had died of starvation. Mother went on to say that Ireland in those days was a harsh place. The potato crop had failed and nothing would grow so many people starved to death.

The box had been given to them by a kind stranger who had helped them when they first arrived in England. The box was plain then – just plain brown panels – but it was all they had. They lived and slept in one room and what few things they had they kept in the box.

They ate their sparse supper sitting on the box and until Eliza grew too big it served as her cot. Every evening her mother would take out the clothes and blankets and she would make a cosy bed inside the chest. Mother would sleep on the floor.

When Charlotte grew up she travelled the world and studied the cultures and religions of the many countries she visited. She noticed the mandala symbol in many eastern countries such as Japan, China, Korea and of course India.

Eliza remembered how she had first noticed the symbol and how Aadi had explained its meaning. It dawned on her that it must have been difficult for Aadi to move to a strange country. His experiences were indeed similar to her Aunt's flight from Ireland. How grateful she was that she had been too young to recall the horrors of that time, though she could remember the musty smell and the wooden walls of her bed in the box.

And so it was that many years later, when times were easier and their lives had flourished, Charlotte commissioned a craftsman to make four carved panels bearing the design of the mandala. This smartened up the plain wooden box but, more importantly, marked the fact that the box had once cradled their few belongings and in those distant days had been the centre of their small universe.

Go to the next page.

1. Which of these phrases best describes the box?

   A   A small cardboard box

   B   A chest of drawers

   C   A box with four cupboards

   D   A beautifully carved chest

   E   A box with initials on it

2. Which word is similar in meaning to 'intricate'?

   A   Complicated

   B   Colourful

   C   Interesting

   D   Curved

   E   Beautiful

3. What type of word is 'wallet'?

   A   Adverb

   B   Verb

   C   Pronoun

   D   Noun

   E   Adjective

4. How did Eliza know about the mandala symbol?

   A   Her great-grandfather told her

   B   The shopkeeper told her

   C   Her mother told her

   D   Aunt Charlotte told her

   E   She was from India

5. What type of word is 'Hyderabad'?

   A   Pronoun

   B   Verb

   C   Proper noun

   D   Adjective

   E   Collective noun

6 Which word is similar in meaning to 'symbol'?

A Motif

B Stamp

C Tattoo

D Letter

E Number

7 Why is the mandala important in India?

A It's a pretty design

B They use it to represent the universe

C They have it on their currency

D It's easy to draw

E It represents flowers

8 Which word is similar in meaning to 'harsh'?

A Lonely

B Harmless

C Hard

D Quiet

E Strange

9 Why did the stranger give them the box?

A The stranger needed to get rid of a box

B The stranger felt sorry for them

C The box was a traditional gift

D Boxes were cheap to make

E Boxes were handy to stand on

10 Which of these phrases best describes why Aunt Charlotte had the mandala symbol carved on the panels?

A To identify it as theirs

B To celebrate her birthday

C To remind them that the box had been very important to them

D To remind them of India

E To match the rest of their furniture

Comprehension Test 20

 You have 8 minutes to complete the following exercise.
You have 10 questions to complete within the time given.

Read the passage and answer the questions that follow.

The Statue

There was a small island in the middle of the duck pond on which there had been a duck house. Over the years the wooden duck dwelling had been slowly rotting away and one morning the park keeper had rowed his little dinghy out to the island and bit by bit taken the broken, crumbly timbers away.

The ducks, geese and rats that lived in the pond were rather disturbed by this activity. They chuntered and complained, whispered and wondered until one sunny afternoon several people arrived at the duck pond.

The creatures of the pond scurried to the further side except for the greedy ducks, who assumed that the visitors would have bread to throw into the pond and insisted on swimming like a flotilla of warships towards the small gathering.

Several visitors kept glaring at their phones, some speaking and then peering down the park drive to the gates. Some of them pointed at the island and some of them took pictures of the pond. The park keeper moved amongst the gathering of people speaking first to one, then another, and the creatures on the island could see that he was also pointing across the pond.

Suddenly one of them said "shush" very loudly and the ducks fled quickly, startled by the sound. Everyone fell silent. In the distance could be heard a rumbling of an empire. A loud chugging engine and an orange-filled light, flashing on and off, penetrated the trees. The creatures of the pond hid themselves in the bushes and reeds of the small island and peered outbetween the fronds of greenery with wide eyes, and every little body quivered with a mixture of anxiety and excitement as the strange noise grew nearer. They all leaned slowly forwards to gain a better view of the thing approaching their usually quiet little community on the island in the pond.

The crowd peered down the park drive as the noise became louder still. Out of the avenue of trees lumbered a huge yellow crane with several orange flashing lights followed by a flathead truck carrying something – an object wrapped in tarpaulin and tied firmly with straps to the back of the lorry.

Slowly and deliberately, the crane moved down the path leading to the pond. The driver, with one hand on the wheel and the other arm resting on the open window, kept leaning sideways so as to gain a clear view of the width of the path. Manoeuvring with precision, he moved gradually towards the perimeter of the pond.

The concealed creatures shook with fright at the strange sight and then watched with ever-increasing curiosity as the crane stopped, and after some adjustments fastened its hook to the object on the truck and slowly and carefully lifted the thing and swung it out and over the pond to where it hung suspended over the island. There the object hung like a giant pupa, the brown wrapping still completely concealing the contents from everyone's view.

The park keeper, with an air of importance, began to pull a yellow and white inflatable dinghy down the grassy bank and across the path towards the pond. Sweating slightly, he pulled a pair of oars from the bottom of the boat which he grasped tightly to his chest as he gently pushed the dinghy into the water and very gingerly stepped on board. After a few seconds, in order to settle himself and to allow the little craft to stabilise, he picked up the oars and with strong pulls moved the boat out into the pond.

The park keeper rowed his dinghy to the island and clambered out. He stuck both thumbs up at the crane driver and immediately the object was lowered down, the park keeper guiding it with his hand until it gently landed on the island. The park keeper pulled the tarpaulin off, as if unwrapping a present, his face now grinning with pleasure, and voila! The statue had arrived!

Go to the next page.

1. Which word is similar in meaning to 'rotting'?

   A   Living

   B   Decaying

   C   Moving

   D   Sailing

   E   Breaking

2. What type of word is 'slowly'?

   A   Noun

   B   Adjective

   C   Pronoun

   D   Adverb

   E   Verb

3. Which of these phrases is similar in meaning to 'rather disturbed by this activity'?

   A   Slightly upset by the event taking place

   B   Unconcerned and relaxed

   C   Enjoying every minute

   D   Unable to sleep

   E   Very excited by everything

4. Which word is similar in meaning to 'chuntered'?

   A   Whispered

   B   Twittered

   C   Grumbled

   D   Laughed

   E   Cackled

5. What type of language device is 'swimming like a flotilla of warships'?

   A   Metaphor

   B   Alliteration

   C   Simile

   D   Clause

   E   Noun

6 What type of language device is the repetition of the initial consonant in 'concealed creatures'?

   A   Simile

   B   Alliteration

   C   Clause

   D   Metaphor

   E   Verb

7 How did the creatures in the passage feel when the crane arrived?

   A   Hungry

   B   Disinterested

   C   Annoyed

   D   Frightened but interested

   E   Overjoyed

8 Which phrase is similar in meaning to 'it hung suspended over the island'?

   A   It flew over the island

   B   It floated to the island

   C   It entered the island

   D   It dangled above the island

   E   It sank under the island

9 Why did the park keeper put his thumbs up to the driver of the crane?

   A   He was judging the wind direction

   B   He had sore thumbs

   C   To signal that he was ready

   D   To signal that the dinghy was sinking

   E   To signal that he wanted him to stop

10 What does 'voila!' mean?

   A   Goodness gracious me!

   B   Go away!

   C   Stop at once!

   D   There it is!

   E   Oh no!

Notes

Acknowledgements

P.14 'For my Grandmother Knitting' by Liz Lochhead from *A Choosing* is reproduced by permission of Polygon, an imprint of Birlinn Ltd (www.birlinn.co.uk).

P.21 Extract from *UK health experts call for ban on tackling in school rugby* by Ben Quinn published 02 March 2016 © Guardian News and Media Ltd 2016. Used by permission.

P.36 *Macavity* by T. S. Eliot, from *Old Possum's Book of Practical Cats* (Faber, 1939). Reprinted by permission of Faber and Faber Ltd.

P.52 Extract from *The 440-million-year-old Scottish fungus which kick-started the human race* by Sarah Knapton published 02 March 2016. © Telegraph Media Group Ltd 2016. Used by permission.

Answers

Comprehension Test 1

Q1 **B**
Everyone would promise to keep the rules

Q2 **E**
Rule one

Q3 **A**
It is the most important rule of all

Q4 **D**
Mixture

Q5 **C**
Being creative is important and you must make something every day

Q6 **E**
Noun

Q7 **C**
Snore

Q8 **A**
Essential

Q9 **B**
Judged

Q10 **E**
Smiles

Comprehension Test 2

Q1 **E**
He had been arrested

Q2 **A**
She didn't want to worry them

Q3 **C**
He wanted to help his Mother as they were now poor

Q4 **C**
When he heard their story, he forgave them

Q5 **D**
Problems

Q6 **C**
Red represents danger and is easily seen

Q7 **E**
There was a landslide on the line

Q8 **B**
With gold pocket watches

Q9 **E**
The truth had been established and Father was innocent

Q10 **D**
He returned to his family

Comprehension Test 3

Q1 **D**
A thrilling and exciting experience

Q2 **B**
A remote and desolate land

Q3 **E**
The effect of not preparing properly could be very serious

Q4 **A**
It is a very remote place with rapidly changing weather

Q5 **D**
The person will get help if you don't come back at the right time

Q6 **C**
Marshy

Q7 **D**
Stones and wooden planks are laid down

Q8 **A**
Lots of different types of hills and drops

Q9 **C**
Manage

Q10 **C**
Noun

Comprehension Test 4

Q1 **E**
She gutted fish

Q2 **B**
Grandmother sometimes finds it hard to understand things

Q3 **B**
Adjective

Q4 **E**
She cut open the fish while it was still wriggling

Q5 **D**
Knitting needles

Q6 **A**
Grandmother's waist was very small

Q7 **C**
They have enough cardigans and scarves

Q8 **B**
Grandmother seemed to have very thin wrists because her hands were so swollen

Q9 *C*

Beat

Q10 *C*

How to stop

Comprehension Test 5

Q1 *D*

Easily set on fire

Q2 *D*

The strong easterly wind

Q3 *E*

Dig

Q4 *C*

They climbed onto the roof

Q5 *B*

A city with closely built buildings and surrounded by countryside

Q6 *A*

They ran to the river and jumped on a boat

Q7 *E*

Tents

Q8 *A*

The flames were too fierce and the wind swept the flames along

Q9 *D*

A large space was made by blowing up some houses

Q10 *B*

The wind lessened

Comprehension Test 6

Q1 *B*

They say tackling can cause serious injuries

Q2 *D*

Most

Q3 *C*

A list of signatures

Q4 *B*

Required

Q5 *A*

That their children will be looked after at school

Q6 *D*

Tag rugby

Q7 *D*

Noun

Q8 *B*

Toughness

Q9 *D*

Collisions

Q10 *B*

They are very careful about player safety

Comprehension Test 7

Q1 *A*

An odd-looking little girl of seven who looked much older

Q2 *C*

Streets

Q3 *E*

Bombay

Q4 *D*

Grown-ups

Q5 *B*

Simile

Q6 *E*

She found them puzzling

Q7 *C*

She was rather anxious

Q8 *D*

He was trying to reassure her

Q9 *B*

She had died

Q10 *B*

She was very fond of him

Comprehension Test 8

Q1 *C*

Adverb

Q2 *B*

A snout and sleepy eyes

Q3 *A*

Hoarse

Q4 *B*

He had probably been on his way to bed

Q5 *D*

They were worn down on the heels

Q6 *C*

He was pleased to see them

Q7 *E*

It was warm and lit by the fire

Q8 *D*

Bundles of dried herbs, hams, onions and eggs

Q9 *C*

Settles, benches and an arm-chair

Q10 *B*

Lines

Comprehension Test 9

Q1 *D*
Noun
Q2 *A*
Basement
Q3 *A*
Verb
Q4 *D*
The land was flat and merged with the sky
Q5 *C*
The sun made the land hard
Q6 *B*
She had a sparkle in her eyes
Q7 *B*
Dorothy's laughter
Q8 *D*
Quiet
Q9 *A*
Adverb
Q10 *E*
Toto

Comprehension Test 10

Q1 *C*
Bewilderment
Q2 *A*
Noun
Q3 *B*
His fur is dirty because he doesn't clean it
Q4 *D*
Simile
Q5 *A*
A demon that looks like a cat
Q6 *D*
They are not found at all
Q7 *A*
He is never there
Q8 *E*
He will be doing long division sums
Q9 *B*
Simple
Q10 *D*
A reason to avoid blame

Comprehension Test 11

Q1 *A*
It gave her the feeling no one knew where she was
Q2 *E*
They were beginning to grow
Q3 *C*
An oddly determined child
Q4 *C*
Engrossed
Q5 *A*
Growing
Q6 *D*
That they spread and made new ones
Q7 *D*
She tried to imagine the flowers
Q8 *D*
All the plants in flower
Q9 *E*
She approached him as quietly as possible
Q10 *C*
He would go away

Comprehension Test 12

Q1 *E*
Neglected and wild
Q2 *C*
Entangled
Q3 *D*
Simile
Q4 *D*
Difference
Q5 *C*
Many creatures inhabited the rooms
Q6 *E*
Alliteration
Q7 *C*
Spiders
Q8 *A*
An indentation in a wall
Q9 *D*
Because slow-worms like to live in the damp and the dark
Q10 *B*
Crowd

Comprehension Test 13

Q1 *C*
In the North country

Q2 *B*
Climb up chimneys

Q3 *D*
Playing with his friends

Q4 *A*
Bravely

Q5 *E*
A master chimney-sweep

Q6 *B*
Simile

Q7 *D*
Tom was a good businessman and always polite to the customers

Q8 *B*
Adjective

Q9 *A*
It disgusted him

Q10 *C*
To suspend fighting

Comprehension Test 14

Q1 *B*
Treasure

Q2 *A*
Dust them

Q3 *C*
They were far too particular

Q4 *D*
He looked over the wall

Q5 *E*
Adjective

Q6 *A*
Laughed

Q7 *E*
He was going in for tea

Q8 *B*
Their dog

Q9 *A*
Noun

Q10 *C*
Proper noun

Comprehension Test 15

Q1 *C*
440 000 000 years old

Q2 *A*
To settle in a place

Q3 *B*
The fungus formed soil

Q4 *E*
Shorter than the width of a human hair

Q5 *B*
Noun

Q6 *D*
Decomposing

Q7 *C*
A petrified impression

Q8 *D*
Sea creatures

Q9 *E*
Sweden and Scotland

Q10 *A*
Adverb

Comprehension Test 16

Q1 *E*
Found the activities very exciting

Q2 *C*
Inept

Q3 *C*
Verb

Q4 *D*
Silver and gold

Q5 *D*
Seventy years

Q6 *B*
They sailed in fleets

Q7 *C*
They flew flags with scary pictures on

Q8 *D*
The pirates were known to be very frightening

Q9 *E*
A flag with skull and crossbones on it

Q10 *C*
In the South China Sea

Comprehension Test 17

Q1 **B**
Simile
Q2 **E**
Eliminated
Q3 **B**
Unhappy
Q4 **A**
Verb
Q5 **B**
His imagination made things seem very alarming
Q6 **E**
The cat jumping on the bench
Q7 **D**
Leather and the neighbour
Q8 **B**
You make it with thoughts
Q9 **B**
Amused because it seemed to be true
Q10 **E**
Imagination can be a good thing or a bad thing

Comprehension Test 18

Q1 **B**
Crowded
Q2 **D**
Look at the roof of the observatory
Q3 **E**
A bright red time ball
Q4 **E**
It falls down the mast
Q5 **C**
You would have to wait 24 hours before you could check the time again
Q6 **A**
They used public sundials
Q7 **B**
There was a variation in time from east to west
Q8 **A**
Placed
Q9 **C**
The observatory had a clock fixed to the gates
Q10 **A**
In Greenwich

Comprehension Test 19

Q1 **D**
A beautifully carved chest
Q2 **A**
Complicated
Q3 **D**
Noun
Q4 **B**
The shopkeeper told her
Q5 **C**
Proper noun
Q6 **A**
Motif
Q7 **B**
They use it to represent the universe
Q8 **C**
Hard
Q9 **B**
The stranger felt sorry for them
Q10 **C**
To remind them that the box had been very important to them

Comprehension Test 20

Q1 **B**
Decaying
Q2 **D**
Adverb
Q3 **A**
Slightly upset by the event taking place
Q4 **C**
Grumbled
Q5 **C**
Simile
Q6 **B**
Alliteration
Q7 **D**
Frightened but interested
Q8 **D**
It dangled above the island
Q9 **C**
To signal that he was ready
Q10 **D**
There it is!

Score Sheet

Below is a score sheet to track your results over multiple attempts. One mark is available for each question in the tests.

Test	Pages	Date of first attempt	Score out of 10	Date of second attempt	Score out of 10	Date of third attempt	Score out of 10
Test 1: School Rules	4–6	25/6/17	8				
Test 2: The Railway Children	7–9						
Test 3: Bloody Bush Mountain Bike Trail	10–13						
Test 4: For my Grandmother Knitting	14–16						
Test 5: The Great Fire of London	17–20						
Test 6: UK health experts call for ban on tackling in school rugby	21–24						
Test 7: The Little Princess	25–28						
Test 8: Mr Badger	29–31						
Tets 9: Cyclone	32–35						
Test 10: Macavity	36–38						
Test 11: Dickon	39–41						
Test 12: The Old House	42–44						
Test 13: Water Babies	45–47						
Test 14: Digging for Treasure	48–51						
Test 15: The 440-million-year-old Scottish fungus which kick-started the human race	52–55						
Test 16: Pirates	56–59						
Test 17: Imagination	60–62						
Test 18: The Greenwich Time Ball	63–65						
Test 19: The Box	66–69						
Test 20: The Statue	70–73						